Bible Verses to Share

Publications International, Ltd.

Scripture quotations marked ERV taken from the *Holy Bible: Easy-to-Read Version (ERV), International Edition*
© 2013, 2016 by Bible League International and used by permission.

All Scripture marked with the designation "GW" is taken from *GOD'S WORD*®.
© 1995, 2003, 2013, 2014, 2019, 2020 by God's Word to the Nations Mission Society.
Used by permission.

Scripture quotations marked KJV are taken from *The Holy Bible, King James Version*.

Scripture quotations marked (TLB) are taken from *The Living Bible*, copyright © 1971 by Tyndale House Foundation. Used by permission of Tyndale House Publishers, Carol Stream, Illinois 60188. All rights reserved.

Scripture quotations marked NRSVUE are taken from the *New Revised Standard Version Updated Edition*. Copyright © 2021 National Council of Churches of Christ in the United States of America. Used by permission. All rights reserved worldwide.

Images from Shutterstock.com
Additional illustrations by Billy Galant

Copyright © 2025 Publications International, Ltd. All rights reserved. This book may not be reproduced or quoted in whole or in part by any means whatsoever without written permission from:

Louis Weber, CEO
Publications International, Ltd.
8140 Lehigh Avenue
Morton Grove, IL 60053

Permission is never granted for commercial purposes.

ISBN: 978-1-63938-817-2

Manufactured in China.

8 7 6 5 4 3 2 1

Let's get social!

@Publications_International

@PublicationsInternational

www.pilbooks.com

Table of Contents

Genesis 1:1, KJV	6	1 Samuel 17:37, KJV	48
Genesis 1:31, KJV	8	1 Kings 3:9, KJV	50
Genesis 2:2, KJV	10	2 Chronicles 6:40, TLB	52
Genesis 2:7, TLB	12	1 Kings 19:11-13, KJV	54
Genesis 6:19-20, TLB	14	2 Kings 4:43, ERV	56
Genesis 9:16, ERV	16	2 Chronicles 31:21, KJV	58
Genesis 17:1, TLB	18	2 Chronicles 34:2, ERV	60
Genesis 18:10, TLB	20	Nehemiah 8:10, KJV	62
Genesis 32:28, ERV	22	Esther 4:16, NRSVUE	64
Genesis 45:4-5, ERV	24	Job 23:11, NRSVUE	66
Exodus 3:14, KJV	26	Psalm 19:1, GW	68
Exodus 4:12, KJV	28	Psalm 23:1, KJV	70
Exodus 13:21, KJV	30	Psalm 96:1, KJV	72
Exodus 14:21-22, KJV	32	Psalm 119:105, KJV	74
Exodus 20:2-3, KJV	34	Proverbs 16:18, TLB	76
Numbers 6:24-26, TLB	36	Proverbs 29:25, ERV	78
Deuteronomy 4:9, TLB	38	Ecclesiastes 3:1, KJV	80
Deuteronomy 6:5, KJV	40	Isaiah 1:18, GW	82
Joshua 1:9, ERV	42	Isaiah 7:14, KJV	84
Ruth 1:16, KJV	44	Isaiah 11:6, TLB	86
1 Samuel 3:10, KJV	46	Isaiah 40:31, KJV	88

Jeremiah 29:11, TLB	90	Matthew 9:9, ERV	136
Lamentations 3:22-23, NRSVUE	92	Matthew 5:1-3, KJV	138
Ezekiel 11:19, KJV	94	Matthew 5:4, KJV	140
Daniel 6:23, ERV	96	Matthew 5:5, KJV	142
Joel 2:12-13, GW	98	Matthew 5:6, KJV	144
Jonah 2:1-2, GW	100	Matthew 5:7, KJV	146
Micah 6:8, ERV	102	Matthew 5:8, KJV	148
Zephaniah 3:17-18, NRSVUE	104	Matthew 5:9, KJV	150
Matthew 1:18-21, ERV	106	Matthew 5:10, KJV	152
Luke 1:13, ERV	108	Matthew 5:14-16, KJV	154
Luke 1:30-31, TLB	110	Matthew 5:43-44, ERV	156
Luke 1:41-42, ERV	112	Matthew 6:1, ERV	158
Luke 2:6-7, GW	114	Matthew 6:9-13, KJV	160
Luke 2:8-9, GW	116	Matthew 6:19-21, ERV	162
Matthew 2:1-2, KJV	118	Matthew 6:26, NRSVUE	164
Matthew 2:11, KJV	120	Matthew 7:1, KJV	166
Luke 2:40, GW	122	Matthew 7:7, KJV	168
Luke 2:46, KJV	124	Matthew 7:12, ERV	170
Matthew 3:1-2, KJV	126	Matthew 12:33, KJV	172
Matthew 3:11, KJV	128	Matthew 18:1-5, ERV	174
Matthew 3:16-17, KJV	130	Matthew 18:21-22, KJV	176
Mark 1:12-13, ERV	132	Matthew 19:13-15, ERV	178
Matthew 4:18-20, TLB	134	Matthew 22:37-40, ERV	180

John 3:16, KJV	182	John 19:30, KJV	228
Mark 1:40-41, TLB	184	Matthew 28:5-7, NRSVUE	230
Luke 4:38-39, ERV	186	John 20:28, KJV	232
Luke 5:18-19, ERV	188	Acts 1:9-11, KJV	234
Mark 5:41-42, GW	190	Acts 2:2-3, ERV	236
Luke 7:6, ERV	192	Acts 9:3-4, ERV	238
Matthew 14:19, ERV	194	Acts 12:6-7, ERV	240
Matthew 14:29-30, ERV	196	1 Corinthians 12:14, KJV	242
Matthew 17:1-2, ERV	198	1 Corinthians 13:13, GW	244
Luke 17:15-18, KJV	200	2 Corinthians 4:7, ERV	246
Matthew 13:34, NRSVUE	202	Galatians 5:22-23, KJV	248
Matthew 13:8, ERV	204	Ephesians 6:1-3, ERV	250
Luke 18:13-14, NRSVUE	206	Ephesians 6:13-14, ERV	252
Matthew 13:31-32, NRSVUE	208	2 Timothy 4:7, ERV	254
Matthew 18:12, TLB	210	Hebrews 11:1, ERV	256
Luke 10:34, TLB	212	James 1:26, ERV	258
Luke 15:20, TLB	214	2 Peter 1:2-3, TLB	260
Luke 15:31-32, TLB	216	1 John 1:5, KJV	262
Luke 19:37, ERV	218	3 John 11, NRSVUE	264
Luke 22:19, GW	220	Revelation 3:20, TLB	266
Luke 22:61, ERV	222	Revelation 4:11, KJV	268
Luke 23:26, GW	224		
Luke 23:42-43, GW	226		

Look around you. Everything that we see, feel, hear, touch, and taste was made by God. God made grand things like the oceans and mountains. God made small things like seashells and pebbles. God created the very ground we walk on and the air we breathe. Every day, we can thank God for the beautiful world he has created and shared with us.

Genesis 1:1

KJV

In the beginning God created the heaven and the earth.

Genesis 1:31

KJV

And God saw every thing that he had made, and, behold, it was very good.

Have you ever colored in a picture or made a sandcastle? It's nice to look at something you made and be happy about it. The creation story in Genesis tells us that God took six days to create our world and everything in it. He created day, night, land, water, plants, the sun, the moon, and the stars. He created birds, fish, whales, snakes, bugs, and all the other animals. Then God looked at what he made and was happy. God loves his creations!

After God worked, he rested. We do the same! People work at jobs, do chores, and go to school. After we work, we need time to rest. We can read, play, and spend time with our family. We spend time with God, too. On the weekend, many people go to church. At church, we stop being busy and take time to remember God and all he has done for us.

Genesis 2:2

KJV

And on the seventh day God ended his work which he had made; and he rested on the seventh day from all his work which he had made.

Genesis 2:7

TLB

The time came when the Lord God formed a man's body from the dust of the ground and breathed into it the breath of life. And man became a living person.

God created you and me! The Bible tells the story of how after God created everything else, he created Adam and Eve, the first humans. God created humans "in his own image." God wants us to be happy and holy and to love God and other people.

The Bible hero Noah and his family were good. They followed God's laws. God sent a big flood over Earth to wipe out bad things, but he wanted to save Noah and his family. He told Noah to build an ark for his family and for a pair of each kind of animal. Noah obeyed God. He built a big ark. The animals went on the ark, two by two.

Genesis 6:19–20

TLB

Bring a pair of every animal—a male and a female—into the boat with you, to keep them alive through the flood. Bring in a pair of each kind of bird and animal and reptile.

Genesis 9:16

ERV

When I look and see the rainbow in the clouds, I will remember the agreement that continues forever. I will remember the agreement between me and every living thing on the earth.

Noah and his family were on the ark for a long time. Finally, it stopped raining and the floodwaters went away. Noah and his family and all the animals left the ark. They prayed to God, and God blessed them. He promised that he would never again send a flood that destroyed everything. He put a rainbow in the sky as a sign of his promise. When we see a rainbow, we can remember God's promise and his love for us.

Abraham was a Bible hero. When he was young, his name was Abram. When he was an old man, God came to him. He wanted Abram to follow him. He promised Abram that God would always be with him to help him and that Abram would be a father and grandfather. God changed Abram's name to Abraham, which means, "father of many nations."

Genesis 17:1
TLB

When Abram was ninety-nine years old, God appeared to him and told him, "I am the Almighty; obey me and live as you should."

Genesis 18:10

TLB

Then the Lord said, "Next year I will give you and Sarah a son!" (Sarah was listening from the tent door behind him.)

Abraham and his wife Sarah did not have any children. But God promised them that they would have a son. Sarah was so surprised that she laughed! She thought she was too old to have a child. With God, though, all things are possible. Abraham and Sarah had a son named Isaac, which means, "he laughs." Don't be afraid to ask God for big things. He can work miracles!

Isaac had two twin sons named Esau and Jacob. They did not get along, and Jacob left home. Later, God told him in a dream that it was time for him to go home. Jacob prayed to God that his brother did not hate him anymore. After that prayer, Jacob saw an angel. They wrestled until the morning. The angel gave Jacob a blessing and a new name. Jacob and Esau forgave each other. God is there to help us through our struggles and to help us forgive each other!

Genesis 32:28

ERV

Then the man said, "Your name will not be Jacob. Your name will now be Israel. I give you this name because you have fought with God and with men, and you have won."

Jacob had twelve sons. He gave his favorite son, Joseph, a coat with many colors. His brothers did not like him. They took his coat and sold him to a group that took him to Egypt. Joseph became an important person in Egypt. During a famine, his brothers came to Egypt to find food. When Joseph met his brothers again, he forgave them and told them God had led him to Egypt. Everything had worked out according to God's plan.

Genesis 45:4–5

ERV

So Joseph said to his brothers again, "Come here to me. I beg you, come here." When the brothers went to him, he said to them, "I am your brother Joseph. I am the one you sold as a slave to Egypt. Now don't be worried. Don't be angry with yourselves for what you did. It was God's plan for me to come here. I am here to save people's lives."

Exodus 3:14

KJV

And God said unto Moses, I AM THAT I AM: and he said, Thus shalt thou say unto the children of Israel, I AM hath sent me unto you.

The people of Jacob, the Israelites, lived in Egypt for many years. The Egyptians began to treat the Israelites as slaves. They were very unhappy. One day, a man named Moses saw a burning bush. God spoke to him from the burning bush. God told Moses that he was the God of his ancestors, Abraham, Isaac, and Jacob. He called Moses to go to Egypt and lead the Israelites out of Egypt to the promised land.

Moses was afraid when God called him. He told God that he was not good at speaking. He did not think the Israelites would follow him. But God told Moses that God would give Moses the right words. We do not need to be perfect to do God's work! God will teach us to say and do the right things, just like he helped Moses.

Exodus 4:12

KJV

Now therefore go, and I will be with thy mouth, and teach thee what thou shalt say.

Exodus 13:21

KJV

And the Lord went before them by day in a pillar of a cloud, to lead them the way; and by night in a pillar of fire, to give them light; to go by day and night.

The Israelites escaped Egypt! They didn't know where to go, so God led them. During the day, the Israelites followed a pillar of a cloud. During the night, they followed a pillar of fire. God always gives us light to follow the path he lays out for us.

While they were escaping Egypt, the Israelites came to the Red Sea. They were afraid. The Egyptians were chasing them. How were they going to cross the sea? But God helped them. When Moses raised his hand, God parted the waters so the Israelites could cross on dry land. What an amazing miracle! Even when things seem hopeless, God has a plan to save us.

Exodus 14:21–22

KJV

And Moses stretched out his hand over the sea; and the Lord caused the sea to go back by a strong east wind all that night, and made the sea dry land, and the waters were divided. And the children of Israel went into the midst of the sea upon the dry ground: and the waters were a wall unto them on their right hand, and on their left.

Exodus 20:2–3

KJV

I am the Lord thy God, which have brought thee out of the land of Egypt, out of the house of bondage. Thou shalt have no other gods before me.

God gave Moses Ten Commandments to give the Israelites. We still learn the Ten Commandments today. They tell us how to follow and obey God. The first commandment is that we should not worship anything or anyone except God. Following God should always be the most important thing in our lives.

This is a beautiful blessing. When we bless someone, we ask for the Lord to give good things to them. You can pray this blessing for someone you love, asking the Lord to protect them, be happy with them, and give them peace.

Numbers 6:24–26

TLB

'May the Lord bless and protect you; may the Lord's face radiate with joy because of you; may he be gracious to you, show you his favor, and give you his peace.'

Deuteronomy 4:9

TLB

Be very careful never to forget what you have seen God doing for you. May his miracles have a deep and permanent effect upon your lives! Tell your children and your grandchildren about the glorious miracles he did.

In the book of Deuteronomy, Moses spoke to the Israelites. After they left Egypt, the Israelites wandered the desert for a very long time before reaching the promised land. Moses reminded the Israelites of how much God had done for them. He told them never to forget about how God saved them from Egypt and led them to the promised land.

God loves us. We're called to love God. Loving God is the most important thing we can do with our lives. In his speech to the Israelites, Moses told them that if they loved and obeyed God, God would continue to give them good things and guide them.

Deuteronomy 6:5

KJV

And thou shalt love the Lord thy God with all thine heart, and with all thy soul, and with all thy might.

Joshua 1:9

ERV

Remember, I commanded you to be strong and brave. Don't be afraid, because the Lord your God will be with you wherever you go.

God spoke these words of comfort to Joshua as he took leadership over the Israelites following Moses' death and prepared to lead them into the promised land. God knew Joshua might feel afraid and discouraged in his new situation, so he revealed a promise that still stands today: God will give you strength and will never leave you.

Ruth 1:16

KJV

And Ruth said, Intreat me not to leave thee, or to return from following after thee: for whither thou goest, I will go; and where thou lodgest, I will lodge: thy people shall be my people, and thy God my God.

The story of Ruth in the Bible is about two women, Ruth and Naomi. Naomi was a Jewish woman who believed in God. Naomi's son married Ruth, who was from a different land. After Naomi's son died, Naomi wanted to go back to her home. She tried to say goodbye to Ruth, but Ruth said she would take care of Naomi, go home with her, and worship Naomi's God. God brings people together, like Ruth and her mother-in-law Naomi!

When Samuel was young, he lived in a temple. In the night, he heard his name called. He did not know it was God calling him. Another prophet, Eli, told him that when he heard God's call, he should answer it. So Samuel did. He became a prophet and a great Bible hero in the times of the kings Saul and David. We too need to listen for God's call.

1 Samuel 3:10

KJV

And the Lord came, and stood, and called as at other times, Samuel, Samuel. Then Samuel answered, Speak; for thy servant heareth.

1 Samuel 17:37

KJV

David said moreover, The Lord that delivered me out of the paw of the lion, and out of the paw of the bear, he will deliver me out of the hand of this Philistine. And Saul said unto David, Go, and the Lord be with thee.

The Israelite army was fighting the Philistines. One of the Philistine fighters, Goliath, was a giant. Everyone was scared of him. David was a young shepherd. He said he would fight Goliath with nothing more than a slingshot. He told King Saul that God had been with him when he protected his sheep from wild animals. He trusted God to be with him now. David won! Like David, we can do great things when we trust God.

David's son Solomon became king after David. Solomon loved God. One night in a dream, God said he would give Solomon anything he asked for. Solomon did not ask for anything for himself, like money or a long life. Instead, he asked for wisdom so he could be a good king. God liked his answer. God said that he would give Solomon wisdom. Because Solomon was not selfish, God gave him riches and honor too!

1 Kings 3:9

KJV

Give therefore thy servant an understanding heart to judge thy people, that I may discern between good and bad: for who is able to judge this thy so great a people?

2 Chronicles 6:40

TLB

Yes, O my God, be wide awake and attentive to all the prayers made to you in this place.

When the Israelites were wandering in the desert, they did not have a temple, a special place to go and pray to the Lord. King Solomon built a grand temple so that people could worship God together. We worship God together when we go to church, and we pray God hears our prayers like he heard Solomon's.

The prophet Elijah was waiting for a message from the Lord. Sometimes God uses big events to get our attention. But other times, God uses small moments. Elijah did not hear God in a strong wind, an earthquake, or a fire, but in a still small voice. We can sit quietly, like Elijah, to hear what God's still small voice tells us.

1 Kings 19:11–13

KJV

And he said, Go forth, and stand upon the mount before the Lord. And, behold, the Lord passed by, and a great and strong wind rent the mountains, and brake in pieces the rocks before the Lord; but the Lord was not in the wind: and after the wind an earthquake; but the Lord was not in the earthquake: And after the earthquake a fire; but the Lord was not in the fire: and after the fire a still small voice. And it was so, when Elijah heard it, that he wrapped his face in his mantle, and went out, and stood in the entering in of the cave. And, behold, there came a voice unto him, and said, What doest thou here, Elijah?

2 Kings 4:43

ERV

Elisha's servant said, "What? There are 100 men here. How can I give this food to all those men?" But Elisha said, "Give the food to the people to eat. The Lord says, 'They will eat and there will still be food left over.'"

In the time of the prophet Elisha, God worked many miracles. One time, there was not food for the men who followed Elisha to eat. Elisha trusted the Lord to provide for them. When they gave the food out, there was enough for everyone. There was even some left over! God gives us many good things when we ask for them. Sometimes he even gives us more than we need!

After David and Solomon, there were many kings. Some were good kings who obeyed God. Others were bad kings who did not obey God. Hezekiah was a good king. Because Hezekiah was a good king, God protected him and healed him when he was sick. We too will prosper, or receive good things, when we seek God with all our heart.

2 Chronicles 31:21

KJV

And in every work that he began in the service of the house of God, and in the law, and in the commandments, to seek his God, he did it with all his heart, and prospered.

2 Chronicles 34:2

ERV

He lived in a way that pleased the Lord, always doing what was right, as his ancestor David had done. Josiah never changed this way of life.

Josiah was another good king. He was only eight years old when he became king! Josiah saw that the people were not worshipping God. He helped the people be faithful to God. He ordered that the temple be repaired. We too can live in a way that pleases the Lord, and be a good example to others.

Following God does not mean we have to be solemn and serious all the time. We can be joyful in our life and our faith. Once, when people were crying during an important holy day, the leader Nehemiah told them to be cheerful and celebrate instead. He said they should have a joyful feast day where they ate and drank together.

Nehemiah 8:10

KJV

The joy of the Lord is your strength.

Esther 4:16

NRSVUE

"Go, gather all the Jews to be found in Susa, and hold a fast on my behalf, and neither eat nor drink for three days, night or day. I and my maids will also fast as you do. After that I will go to the king, though it is against the law, and if I perish, I perish."

Esther was a queen. One time, the Jewish people were in great danger because the king's adviser hated them. Esther was very brave. She decided to ask the king to change his mind. Before she took action, Esther prayed and fasted, and said everyone else should too. Then she went to the king and pleaded for her people. The king listened to her and the Jewish people were saved!

Job went through a very hard time in his life. He lost his flocks of animals. He became ill. Worst of all, his children died. Some of Job's friends thought God must be punishing him. But Job knew that he had kept faith with God and followed God's ways. He never stopped believing in God, even during hard times. Like Job, we need to keep faith both when things are going well and when we are going through hard times.

Job 23:11

NRSVUE

My foot has held fast to his steps; I have kept his way and have not turned aside.

Psalm 19:1
GW

The heavens declare the glory of God, and the sky displays what his hands have made.

The book of Psalms contains many beautiful songs and poems. In the Psalms, people pray directly to God to praise him, thank him, and ask him for forgiveness. This verse reminds us to look around at God's amazing creation. In the day, we can see sky and clouds. In the night, we can see stars. All of these are God's work!

God is like a shepherd who takes care of his sheep. He makes sure we have what we need. He protects us. He guides us. He leads us to live the right way. When we follow God, we do not need to be afraid.

Psalm 23:1

KJV

The Lord is my shepherd; I shall not want.

Psalm 96:1

KJV

O sing unto the Lord a new song: sing unto the Lord, all the earth.

Music is one way to praise God! You can sing, clap your hands, and dance to praise God and give thanks for how good he is. You can sing along with the sounds nature makes: birds chirping, frogs croaking, ocean waves crashing, and the wind blowing.

Just like a lamp in the dark, God's Word helps you see where to go and what to do. Without God's Word, you're likely to stumble and fall. The Bible reveals the truth about God and people so you can make wise decisions. God's Word can comfort you, guide you, and serve as your ultimate self-improvement manual.

Psalm 119:105

KJV

Thy word is a lamp unto my feet, and a light unto my path.

Proverbs 16:18

TLB

Pride goes before destruction and haughtiness before a fall.

The book of Proverbs has a lot of advice to tell us how to live in a way that pleases God. This proverb says that pride goes before a fall. All our abilities are gifts from God. When we get too proud, we forget that. We think we can do things on our own. It never works out in the long run, though. Sooner or later, our pride means we mess up and everything goes wrong.

Everybody gets afraid sometimes. Sadly, our fear can keep us from doing things we need to do. God tells us that we don't need to be afraid. We can trust in him. He will keep us safe from harm. What a wonderful gift!

Proverbs 29:25

ERV

Fear can be a trap, but if you trust in the Lord, you will be safe.

Ecclesiastes 3:1

KJV

To every thing there is a season, and a time to every purpose under the heaven.

This verse tells us that there is a time for everything. Sometimes we will be sad. Sometimes we will be happy. Sometimes it is time to plant crops like corn and wheat. Sometimes it is time to gather the full-grown plants so we can eat them. Sometimes we should talk, and sometimes we should be silent. God is with us at all times.

Imagine that you spilled paint all over your clothes. You would worry that they were ruined. The paint would never come out! But God could make them clean again, so you wouldn't even see a stain. Our mistakes and sins are like that paint. We feel bad when we do bad things, but God promises that he forgives us completely.

Isaiah 1:18

GW

"Come on now, let's discuss this!" says the Lord. "Though your sins are bright red, they will become as white as snow. Though they are dark red, they will become as white as wool."

Isaiah 7:14

KJV

Therefore the Lord himself shall give you a sign; Behold, a virgin shall conceive, and bear a son, and shall call his name Immanuel.

Prophets like Isaiah told the people what God wanted and how to live. They told people God's promises for what would happen. Many years before Jesus was born, God made a promise that someday a virgin would bear a son and name him Immanuel. Immanuel means, "God is with us." Jesus is the fulfillment of that prophecy. He is always with us!

The prophet Isaiah talked about a Messiah, a great leader who would lead the people to peace. Even animals that were normally enemies would get along. That seems impossible, but with God, everything is possible. God wants everyone to be at peace with each other, following God's laws.

Isaiah 11:6
TLB

In that day the wolf and the lamb will lie down together, and the leopard and goats will be at peace. Calves and fat cattle will be safe among lions, and a little child shall lead them all.

Isaiah 40:31

KJV

But they that wait upon the Lord shall renew their strength; they shall mount up with wings as eagles; they shall run, and not be weary; and they shall walk, and not faint.

Sometimes it is hard to do God's work. You can get tired or think you do not have the strength to do the right thing. God promises that he will give you that strength, as if you could run without getting tired or out of breath.

God loves each of us. He has plans for each of us. God's plans for you are not the same as his plans for anyone else, because you are special in his eyes. We can pray that we will listen to and follow God's plans for us, knowing that they are good, hopeful plans.

Jeremiah 29:11

TLB

For I know the plans I have for you, says the Lord. They are plans for good and not for evil, to give you a future and a hope.

Lamentations 3:22–23

NRSVUE

The steadfast love of the Lord never ceases, his mercies never come to an end; they are new every morning; great is your faithfulness.

God never stops loving you. Even if you forget to pray at night, or do something bad, God does not stop loving you. He is faithful to you. That means he keeps his promises to you. He does not forget about you or grow tired of you.

The prophet Ezekiel was talking to people who had stopped following God. They had hard hearts. When they did bad things, they were not sorry about it. But God said they could turn back to him. He would make their heart soft, so they could love God and be forgiven. God wants us to have soft, loving hearts.

Ezekiel 11:19

KJV

And I will give them one heart, and I will put a new spirit within you; and I will take the stony heart out of their flesh, and will give them an heart of flesh.

Daniel 6:23

ERV

King Darius was very happy. He told his servants to lift Daniel out of the lions' den. And when Daniel was lifted out of the den, they did not find any injury on his body. The lions did not hurt Daniel because he trusted in his God.

The Bible hero Daniel worked for a king named Darius. A new law said that people needed to pray only to King Darius. If they prayed to anyone else, they would be punished. Daniel loved God and kept praying to him, because he knew that was the right thing to do. Because of that, Daniel was put in a big den with lions! But since Daniel was faithful to God, God was faithful to him. God saved him from the lions!

In Bible times, when people were very sad or very sorry about something, they would tear their own clothes. That way, anyone who looked at them would see their sadness or guilt. God doesn't want us to put on a big show of being sorry for our sins, though. He wants us to be sorry deep in our hearts, instead of putting on an outward show.

Joel 2:12–13

GW

"But even now," declares the LORD, "return to me with all your heart— with fasting, crying, and mourning." Tear your hearts, not your clothes. Return to the LORD your God. He is merciful and compassionate, patient, and always ready to forgive and to change his plans about disaster.

Jonah 2:1–2

GW

From inside the fish Jonah prayed to the Lord his God. Jonah prayed:
"I called to the Lord in my distress,
and he answered me.
From the depths of my watery grave I cried for help,
and you heard my cry.

God told the prophet Jonah to deliver God's message to Nineveh. Jonah did not want to. He ran away and got on a boat. God stirred up a big storm, and Jonah was swallowed by a big fish. Inside the fish, Jonah repented for not doing God's will. He prayed to God to save him. God did! Jonah went on to Nineveh, and the people of Nineveh heard God's message and repented of the bad things they were doing.

How do we know what to do to be good? The Bible tells us. God wants us to be fair. We should not treat some people one way and other people another way. God wants us to be kind to others. We should help other people and not be mean to them. God wants us to listen to him and obey him.

Micah 6:8

ERV

The Lord has told you what goodness is. This is what he wants from you: Be fair to other people. Love kindness and loyalty, and humbly obey your God.

Zephaniah 3:17–18

NRSVUE

The Lord, your God, is in your midst, a warrior who gives victory; he will rejoice over you with gladness; he will renew you in his love; he will exult over you with loud singing as on a day of festival.

You make God happy! When you do something good, God is happy about it. He cheers you on like you are an athlete who is running a race. He is proud of you and loves you!

The Gospels tell the good news of how Jesus came to save us! God the father sent his son Jesus to be human and live among us. God sent Jesus to Mary and Joseph to take care of him as a baby. Joseph did not know what to do when he thought Mary was having a baby with someone else. But he had a dream and realized that the baby was God's special son.

Matthew 1:18–21

ERV

This is how the birth of Jesus the Messiah happened. His mother Mary was engaged to marry Joseph. But before they married, he learned that she was expecting a baby. (She was pregnant by the power of the Holy Spirit.) Mary's husband, Joseph, was a good man. He did not want to cause her public disgrace, so he planned to divorce her secretly.

But after Joseph thought about this, an angel from the Lord came to him in a dream. The angel said, "Joseph, son of David, don't be afraid to accept Mary to be your wife. The baby inside her is from the Holy Spirit. She will give birth to a son. You will name him Jesus. Give him that name because he will save his people from their sins."

Luke 1:13

ERV

But the angel said to him, "Zechariah, don't be afraid. Your prayer has been heard by God. Your wife Elizabeth will give birth to a baby boy, and you will name him John.

The Bible tells the story of how the angel Gabriel appeared to a man named Zechariah to tell him he would have a son, and that son would be a great prophet. Zechariah was surprised since he and his wife Elizabeth were old. But the angel was right! Zechariah and Elizabeth had a baby boy. That baby grew up to be John the Baptist, who told everyone that Jesus was coming.

When an angel appeared to Mary, she was surprised and troubled. Mary was young. She was engaged to Joseph and looking forward to their life together. She did not expect to see an angel that day with news that would change her life! But Mary was obedient. She said she was the Lord's servant and would do what God wanted. She said yes to God's plan!

Luke 1:30–31

TLB

"Don't be frightened, Mary," the angel told her, "for God has decided to wonderfully bless you! Very soon now, you will become pregnant and have a baby boy, and you are to name him 'Jesus.'

Luke 1:41–42

ERV

When Elizabeth heard Mary's greeting, the unborn baby inside her jumped, and she was filled with the Holy Spirit.

In a loud voice she said to Mary, "God has blessed you more than any other woman. And God has blessed the baby you will have."

Mary and Elizabeth were related. Mary went to visit Elizabeth when they were both pregnant. When Elizabeth saw Mary, the baby in her womb leapt. Elizabeth suddenly knew that the baby that Mary was carrying would be special. Elizabeth knew that God was working, and gave praise to God. Just like Elizabeth, we can give praise to God when we see him at work.

Mary and Joseph had to travel to Bethlehem right before Jesus was born. It must have been a hard journey. They had nowhere to stay when they got to Bethlehem, so they had to stay in a stable. Jesus was not born in a palace with lots of things. Instead, he was born in a small town, in a lowly place, and placed in the trough that animals used for food. God can do great things in unexpected places!

Luke 2:6–7

GW

While they were in Bethlehem, the time came for Mary to have her child. She gave birth to her firstborn son. She wrapped him in strips of cloth and laid him in a manger because there wasn't any room for them in the inn.

Luke 2:8–9

GW

Shepherds were in the fields near Bethlehem. They were taking turns watching their flock during the night. An angel from the Lord suddenly appeared to them. The glory of the Lord filled the area with light, and they were terrified.

Shepherds were humble men who took care of their sheep. When they saw an angel, they were frightened! But the angel told them not to be afraid. The angel told them to visit Jesus. The shepherds did, and then they told people about what they had seen. These humble men were some of the earliest people to spread the gospel, the good news, of Jesus' coming.

Jesus was born to a Jewish family, but he came to save the whole world. Wise men, or magi, from far-off lands saw a star. They knew it meant something special was happening. They traveled a long way to find Jesus. Whatever country people come from, God welcomes them when they come to him.

Matthew 2:1–2

KJV

Now when Jesus was born in Bethlehem of Judaea in the days of Herod the king, behold, there came wise men from the east to Jerusalem, Saying, Where is he that is born King of the Jews? for we have seen his star in the east, and are come to worship him.

Matthew 2:11

KJV

And when they were come into the house, they saw the young child with Mary his mother, and fell down, and worshipped him: and when they had opened their treasures, they presented unto him gifts; gold, and frankincense and myrrh.

The wise men brought special, costly treasures for Jesus. Gold was a gift fit for kings, because Jesus was the king of kings. Frankincense smells good when it is burned. It was used in temples to worship God. Myrrh is a spice that smells good. People used it as a perfume. All of these gifts pointed towards how important Jesus was. We can give Jesus good gifts of praise and thanks.

Jesus was a little child, just like you! The Bible does not say a lot about what Jesus' childhood was like. Just like kids today, he would have learned from his parents, played games, and laughed! He would have learned about God's laws and how God helped people like Abraham, Isaac, Jacob, and Moses.

Luke 2:40

GW

The child grew and became strong. He was filled with wisdom, and God's favor was with him.

Luke 2:46
KJV

And it came to pass, that after three days they found him in the temple, sitting in the midst of the doctors, both hearing them, and asking them questions.

When Jesus was twelve, he and his family went to Jerusalem for a feast day. When they were going home, Mary and Joseph found out that they did not know where Jesus was! They went back to Jerusalem and found him there in the temple. Even though Jesus was young, he was able to talk to the elders and teachers there, and they listened to his wisdom.

Before Jesus went out in the world, the prophet John the Baptist began to preach and prepare the way for Jesus. John lived a simple life. He ate locusts and wild honey. He told people to be sorry and repent for their sins. We still listen to John's message today. We can pray and prepare for Jesus to be in our life.

Matthew 3:1–2

KJV

In those days came John the Baptist, preaching in the wilderness of Judaea, And saying, Repent ye: for the kingdom of heaven is at hand.

Matthew 3:11

KJV

I indeed baptize you with water unto repentance. but he that cometh after me is mightier than I, whose shoes I am not worthy to bear: he shall baptize you with the Holy Ghost, and with fire.

John the Baptist baptized people in the Jordan River. They were baptized as a symbol to show they were sorry for their sins. Baptism washed away their sins like water washes away dirt. John told people that another person greater than him would follow him. Jesus was coming!

Jesus went to John the Baptist to be baptized. John was surprised. He said Jesus did not need to be baptized. Jesus was already holy! But Jesus wanted to be baptized. When John baptized Jesus, the Holy Spirit came down! People heard the voice of God telling everyone that Jesus was his son.

Matthew 3:16–17

KJV

And Jesus, when he was baptized, went up straightway out of the water: and, lo, the heavens were opened unto him, and he saw the Spirit of God descending like a dove, and lighting upon him: And lo a voice from heaven, saying, This is my beloved Son, in whom I am well pleased.

Mark 1:12–13

ERV

Then the Spirit sent Jesus into the desert alone. He was there for 40 days, being tempted by Satan. During this time he was out among the wild animals. Then angels came and helped him.

After Jesus was baptized, he went out into the desert. This was a hard, lonely time. The devil tempted Jesus, saying he would give Jesus the world if Jesus would worship him. Jesus refused. When we are tempted to sin, we can try to be like Jesus. We can ask for God's help in resisting temptation, and thank God for his protection.

Jesus called some people to travel with him and help him with his work in a special way. They were the apostles, and there were twelve of them. Peter and Andrew both became apostles. When Jesus called them, they knew right away that they wanted to follow him. Everyone has a call to serve God. Not everyone is called to serve God in the same way, but we should all follow our call like Peter and Andrew did.

Matthew 4:18–20

TLB

One day as he was walking along the beach beside the Lake of Galilee, he saw two brothers—Simon, also called Peter, and Andrew—out in a boat fishing with a net, for they were commercial fishermen. Jesus called out, "Come along with me and I will show you how to fish for the souls of men!" And they left their nets at once and went with him.

Matthew 9:9

ERV

When Jesus was leaving, he saw a man named Matthew sitting at the place for collecting taxes. Jesus said to him, "Follow me." So he got up and followed Jesus.

Matthew was another one of the apostles. He was a tax collector. Other people did not like tax collectors, because many tax collectors were not nice people. But Jesus called someone that other people saw as a sinner to be his follower. We do not need to be perfect to follow Jesus!

Jesus was a great teacher. He told people how to live in ways that please God. Jesus told people about a set of beatitudes, or blessings. People who follow the beatitudes will be happy and blessed by God. The first beatitude says to be poor in spirit, or humble. People who rely on God and give him control will be honored in heaven.

Matthew 5:1–3

KJV

And seeing the multitudes, he went up into a mountain: and when he was set, his disciples came unto him: And he opened his mouth, and taught them, saying, Blessed are the poor in spirit: for theirs is the kingdom of heaven.

Matthew 5:4

KJV

Blessed are they that mourn: for they shall be comforted.

Usually we do not want to be sad, to cry, or to mourn. But this beatitude says that people who mourn will be blessed, because God will comfort them. God takes care of us, even in the middle of sadness.

This beatitude says that the meek will be blessed. People who are meek are gentle. They are patient and humble. They are slow to anger and have control over their emotions. Later in the Bible, Jesus called himself "meek and lowly in heart" (Matthew 11:29). When we are tempted to be mean or yell to get our way, we can remind ourselves to be meek instead.

Matthew 5:5

KJV

Blessed are the meek: for they shall inherit the earth.

Matthew 5:6

KJV

Blessed are they which do hunger and thirst after righteousness: for they shall be filled.

This beatitude blesses people who want to do right. Some people want things to be fair, right, and just. They hunger and thirst for it, like it is as important and necessary as food. This beatitude promises that God will satisfy them.

Jesus talked about mercy and forgiveness many times. We all sin and need to be forgiven. We all need mercy from God. Just like God is merciful and forgives us, we need to be merciful and forgive each other.

Matthew 5:7

KJV

Blessed are the merciful: for they shall obtain mercy.

Matthew 5:8

KJV

Blessed are the pure in heart: for they shall see God.

This beatitude says that the pure in heart will see God. People who are pure in heart put God first. They focus on what God wants for them and try to do what God wants them to do. They don't get distracted by the world, and they avoid sinful thoughts and acts. God stays close to the people who want to be close to him!

This beatitude promises that peacemakers will be blessed. God does not want us to argue and be mad all the time, or mean to others. He wants people to be at peace with God and each other. Peacemakers help other people love and forgive. God thinks of peacemakers as his children.

Matthew 5:9

KJV

Blessed are the peacemakers: for they shall be called the children of God.

Matthew 5:10

KJV

Blessed are they which are persecuted for righteousness' sake: for theirs is the kingdom of heaven.

We don't like it when someone is mean to us! But if someone is mean to us because of our faith in God, and we still have faith, then we will be blessed. Many of the Bible heroes were persecuted for their faith, like Daniel, who was thrown into the lions' den. Like them, we can be brave, knowing that God will bless and reward us.

A good person is like a bright, shining light in the middle of darkness. Jesus told us not to hide our good deeds or our love of God, just like you would not hide a light by putting it in a bushel or bucket. Our faith can set a good example for other people, so they can shine too.

Matthew 5:14–16

KJV

Ye are the light of the world. A city that is set on an hill cannot be hid. Neither do men light a candle, and put it under a bushel, but on a candlestick; and it giveth light unto all that are in the house. Let your light so shine before men, that they may see your good works, and glorify your Father which is in heaven.

Matthew 5:43–44

ERV

You have heard that it was said, 'Love your neighbor and hate your enemy.' But I tell you, love your enemies. Pray for those who treat you badly.

It can be hard to be kind and loving to people who are not acting kind and loving to you. God loves everyone, though, and he wants us to love and forgive people just as he loves and forgives them. When it is hard to love, we can pray to God and ask for his help.

Sometimes people do good things not because it's the right thing to do, but so they can brag about it. Jesus taught that we should not brag about doing good things. Instead, we should just do them. God sees everything, and he sees when we do good things, and rewards us for them.

Matthew 6:1

ERV

Be careful! When you do something good, don't do it in front of others so that they will see you. If you do that, you will have no reward from your Father in heaven.

Matthew 6:9–13

KJV

After this manner therefore pray ye: Our Father which art in heaven, Hallowed be thy name.
Thy kingdom come, Thy will be done in earth, as it is in heaven.
Give us this day our daily bread.
And forgive us our debts, as we forgive our debtors.
And lead us not into temptation, but deliver us from evil: For thine is the kingdom, and the power, and the glory, for ever. Amen.

Jesus taught his followers how to pray. We still say the prayer Jesus taught today. The Lord's Prayer praises God the Father. It asks that everything be done according to God's will. It asks that God give us what we need to get through the day. It reminds us to forgive others and asks God to forgive any sins. It asks that God protect us from everything bad.

We have lots of things: toys, clothes, books, and decorations. These things are not bad, but they are not as important as obeying God and doing good things. Jesus taught that it is better to learn about God and be kind to others than to have many possessions. Things get old and worn out, but God's love never wears out.

Matthew 6:19–21

ERV

Don't save treasures for yourselves here on earth. Moths and rust will destroy them. And thieves can break into your house and steal them. Instead, save your treasures in heaven, where they cannot be destroyed by moths or rust and where thieves cannot break in and steal them. Your heart will be where your treasure is.

Matthew 6:26

NRSVUE

Look at the birds of the air: they neither sow nor reap nor gather into barns, and yet your heavenly Father feeds them. Are you not of more value than they?

God made every flower, bird, and tree. He feeds them and makes them grow. If God takes such good care of these little things, you can trust he'll take good care of you. You are much more important than birds or flowers. Don't worry about anything. God will make sure you have what you need. Take your worries to God in prayer and then let them go.

Sometimes we think mean things about other people. We think that we are better than them. Jesus taught us that if we judge other people harshly, we will be judged harshly. We all sin and need God's forgiveness, mercy, and grace.

Matthew 7:1

KJV

Judge not, that ye be not judged.

Matthew 7:7

KJV

Ask, and it shall be given you; seek, and ye shall find; knock, and it shall be opened unto you.

Jesus taught that God wants to give good things to us. When we ask for those good things, God will surely grant them, just like God gave wisdom to King Solomon when he asked for it. Jesus said that just like a father wouldn't give a stone to a son who asked for bread, God won't give us bad things, but "good gifts."

Just as you would want others to be kind to you, you should be kind to others. Just as you would want others to forgive you when you do something wrong, you should forgive others. Just as you would want help if you were hurt, you should help others.

Matthew 7:12

ERV

Do for others what you would want them to do for you. This is the meaning of the Law of Moses and the teaching of the prophets.

Matthew 12:33

KJV

Either make the tree good, and his fruit good; or else make the tree corrupt, and his fruit corrupt: for the tree is known by his fruit.

If we do good deeds because we love God, we are like a tree that produces good fruit instead of rotten fruit. Our love for God is reflected in our actions and our words. We won't always be perfect, but we want people to be able to see how much we love God by how we act.

In the eyes of the world, the most important people might be leaders, presidents, musicians, or actors. God sees differently, though. The greatest people in God's eyes are those people who love and serve God humbly. You do not have to be powerful or do great things in the world's eyes for God to love you and for you to love God.

Matthew 18:1–5

ERV

About that time the followers came to Jesus and asked, "Who is the greatest in God's kingdom?" Jesus called a little child to come to him. He stood the child in front of the followers. Then he said, "The truth is, you must change your thinking and become like little children. If you don't do this, you will never enter God's kingdom. The greatest person in God's kingdom is the one who makes himself humble like this child. "Whoever accepts a little child like this in my name is accepting me.

Matthew 18:21–22

KJV

Then came Peter to him, and said, Lord, how oft shall my brother sin against me, and I forgive him? till seven times? Jesus saith unto him, I say not unto thee, Until seven times: but, Until seventy times seven.

Seventy times seven is four hundred ninety times. That's a lot of times to forgive someone! It can be hard to forgive people, especially people who have hurt us before. It can be easier to forgive others, though, if we remember how many times God forgives us for our sins.

Some of Jesus' followers tried to stop children from coming to Jesus. They thought children were not important or serious enough for Jesus to pay attention to them. Jesus wanted to meet the children, though. He loves everyone, young or old. Whatever your age, you are important to Jesus, and he loves you!

Matthew 19:13–15

ERV

Then the people brought their little children to Jesus so that he could lay his hands on them to bless them and pray for them. When the followers saw this, they told the people to stop bringing their children to him. But Jesus said, "Let the little children come to me. Don't stop them, because God's kingdom belongs to people who are like these children." After Jesus blessed the children, he left there.

Matthew 22:37–40

ERV

Jesus answered, "'Love the Lord your God with all your heart, all your soul, and all your mind.' This is the first and most important command. And the second command is like the first: 'Love your neighbor the same as you love yourself.' All of the law and the writings of the prophets take their meaning from these two commands."

Some powerful people did not like Jesus because they worried that if people listened to Jesus, people would not listen to them. They asked him tricky questions, hoping that Jesus would say something wrong that would make people stop listening to him. A lawyer asked Jesus what the greatest commandment was, since there were hundreds of them. Jesus quoted the scriptures that said to love God and love your neighbor. No one could argue with that.

An important man named Nicodemus wanted to learn from Jesus. He met Jesus at night and asked him many questions. Jesus told Nicodemus that God sent his son to save the world. Those who believe in Jesus will someday have eternal life in heaven.

John 3:16

KJV

For God so loved the world, that he gave his only begotten Son, that whosoever believeth in him should not perish, but have everlasting life.

Mark 1:40–41

TLB

Once a leper came and knelt in front of him and begged to be healed. "If you want to, you can make me well again," he pled.

And Jesus, moved with pity, touched him and said, "I want to! Be healed!"

Jesus worked many miracles as signs of God's power. He healed people who were sick, drove out demons that were hurting people, and calmed storms. One of his miracles was healing a leper. Leprosy was a bad skin disease that was contagious. Lepers could not live with other people. A leper asked Jesus for help. Jesus wanted him to be well and whole, and so he healed him. Jesus wants us to be well and whole, too!

Another miracle Jesus performed was when he healed the mother-in-law of his apostle Simon Peter. She was grateful to be healed and got up to serve them. When we are healthy, we can thank God for our good health, and get up and serve God too!

Luke 4:38–39

ERV

Jesus left the synagogue and went to Simon's house. Simon's mother-in-law was very sick. She had a high fever. They asked Jesus to do something to help her. He stood very close to her and ordered the sickness to go away. The sickness left her, and she got up and began serving them.

Luke 5:18–19

ERV

There was a man who was paralyzed, and some other men were carrying him on a mat. They tried to bring him and put him down before Jesus. But there were so many people that they could not find a way to Jesus. So they went up on the roof and lowered the crippled man down through a hole in the ceiling. They lowered the mat into the room so that the crippled man was lying before Jesus.

The paralyzed man could not walk or move on his own. His friends had to help him reach Jesus. Jesus told the man his sins were forgiven. He also told the man to stand up and go home. Right away, the man was able to stand up and walk! We can help our friends, and our friends can help us, by praying for each other. We can share stories of God with each other. We can help each other get closer to Jesus, just like the man's friends helped him!

A man named Jairus had a daughter who was sick. Jairus went to find Jesus and ask him to heal his daughter, and Jesus agreed to come and help. As they were going to Jairus's house, some men came. They said that Jairus's daughter had died, and Jesus could not do anything to help her. Jesus told Jairus to have faith. Then he raised Jairus's daughter from the dead and told her parents to give the little girl something to eat. Jesus can always help, even when it seems impossible!

Mark 5:41–42

GW

Jesus took the child's hand and said to her, "Talitha, koum!" which means, "Little girl, I'm telling you to get up!"

The girl got up at once and started to walk. (She was twelve years old.) They were astonished.

Luke 7:6

ERV

So Jesus went with them. He was coming near the officer's house when the officer sent friends to say, "Lord, you don't need to do anything special for me. I am not good enough for you to come into my house.

One day, some Jewish leaders came to Jesus. They asked for help for a Roman army officer who was good to the Jewish people. The officer's servant was sick, and the officer wanted Jesus to heal him. Jesus agreed. The officer sent a friend to tell Jesus that he did not need to travel all the way to the officer's house. He believed Jesus could heal his servant even from far away! Jesus was very impressed by his faith, and he healed the servant.

Once, a big crowd of people came to meet Jesus. Jesus' followers told Jesus to send the crowd away, because there was not enough food. There were only five loaves of bread and two fish. Jesus said to bring the food to him. He prayed over it. When they passed out the food, everyone had enough to eat. There were even twelve baskets of food left over! God provides what we need when we trust in him.

Matthew 14:19

ERV

Then he told the people to sit down on the grass. He took the five loaves of bread and the two fish. He looked into the sky and thanked God for the food. Then he broke the bread into pieces, which he gave to the followers, and they gave the food to the people.

Matthew 14:29–30

ERV

Jesus said, "Come, Peter."

Then Peter left the boat and walked on the water to Jesus. But while Peter was walking on the water, he saw the wind and the waves. He was afraid and began sinking into the water. He shouted, "Lord, save me!"

One night the apostles were out in a boat on the water. Jesus was not there. The waves started getting higher. The apostles saw a figure walking towards them on the rough water. They thought it was a ghost! They were scared, but then they realized it was Jesus, walking on water. He told them not to be afraid. Peter left the boat and walked on water to meet Jesus. Then he got scared. He started to sink. Jesus saved him and told Peter to have faith and not to doubt. When we have a strong faith in Jesus, we can do amazing things.

One day, Jesus took three of his apostles up a mountain to see a very special moment when God revealed his glory. On the mountain, Jesus was changed, or transfigured. Peter, James, and John saw the Bible heroes Elijah and Moses join Jesus. They heard the voice of God saying Jesus was his son! The Transfiguration showed God's awesome power.

Matthew 17:1–2

ERV

Jesus took Peter, James, and John the brother of James and went up on a high mountain. They were all alone there. While these followers watched him, Jesus was changed. His face became bright like the sun, and his clothes became white as light.

Luke 17:15–18

KJV

And one of them, when he saw that he was healed, turned back, and with a loud voice glorified God, And fell down on his face at his feet, giving him thanks: and he was a Samaritan. And Jesus answering said, Were there not ten cleansed? but where are the nine? There are not found that returned to give glory to God, save this stranger.

One day, Jesus healed ten lepers. One of them was a Samaritan. The Samaritans and the Jews did not always get along, but Jesus healed the Samaritan man just the same as the others. The Samaritan man was the only one who came back to thank Jesus! Sometimes when things go well, we are so happy that we forget to thank God. It's good to remember to say "thank you" to God for the gifts he gives us!

When Jesus was teaching people, he used stories called parables. Parables were often simple stories about everyday life, or things that might happen to people. Parables made it easy for people to understand the lessons Jesus was trying to teach.

Matthew 13:34

NRSVUE

Jesus told the crowds all these things in parables; without a parable he told them nothing.

Matthew 13:8

ERV

But some of the seed fell on good ground. There it grew and made grain. Some plants made 100 times more grain, some 60 times more, and some 30 times more.

Jesus told a parable about a man who threw seeds on the ground. Some seeds got eaten up by birds. Some seeds fell on rocky ground, and the plants that grew died quickly because there was no soil. Some seeds fell on thorns, and plants could not grow. But some seed fell on good soil. Jesus explained that God's Word is like that seed. Sometimes it cannot grow because of sin or distractions. We can pray that our heart is good soil so that God's Word can grow.

Jesus told a parable about two men who went to pray at the temple. One was a Pharisee, a man who knew religious laws. The other was a tax collector. When the Pharisee prayed, he bragged about how good he was in comparison to other people. The tax collector admitted he was a sinner and asked for God's mercy. Jesus said that God would rather hear the tax collector's prayer.

Luke 18:13–14

NRSVUE

But the tax collector, standing far off, would not even lift up his eyes to heaven but was beating his breast and saying, 'God, be merciful to me, a sinner!' I tell you, this man went down to his home justified rather than the other, for all who exalt themselves will be humbled, but all who humble themselves will be exalted."

Matthew 13:31–32

NRSVUE

He put before them another parable: "The kingdom of heaven is like a mustard seed that someone took and sowed in his field; it is the smallest of all the seeds, but when it has grown it is the greatest of shrubs and becomes a tree, so that the birds of the air come and make nests in its branches."

Great things can come from small beginnings, just like big trees can come from small seeds. Every action we take, even ones that do not seem important, can help us build our faith. And God can use small things and unimportant people to build the kingdom of heaven!

Jesus told a parable about a lost sheep. The shepherd left his other sheep to find the lost one. In the same way, Jesus came to save sinners, the people who need him most. He is the Good Shepherd who rejoices when he saves his sheep!

Matthew 18:12

TLB

"If a man has a hundred sheep, and one wanders away and is lost, what will he do? Won't he leave the ninety-nine others and go out into the hills to search for the lost one?

Luke 10:34

TLB

Kneeling beside him the Samaritan soothed his wounds with medicine and bandaged them. Then he put the man on his donkey and walked along beside him till they came to an inn, where he nursed him through the night.

Someone asked Jesus how to gain eternal life. Jesus reminded him to follow the law by loving God and his neighbor. The man asked who was his neighbor. Jesus told the parable of the Good Samaritan as an answer. A man was robbed and hurt by thieves. The only person who helped was a Samaritan, even though Samaritans and Jews did not always get along. The Samaritan acted as a good and loving neighbor.

Jesus told the parable of the Prodigal Son. A man had two sons. One helped his father. The other son asked his father for money so he could go away. When he was away, he did not obey God's laws. Then everything went wrong. The son lost his money. He decided to return home and say sorry to his father. He would offer to live as a servant in his father's house. But his father forgave him completely. He even threw him a party! The father loved his son, just like God loves us.

Luke 15:20

TLB

"So he returned home to his father. And while he was still a long distance away, his father saw him coming, and was filled with loving pity and ran and embraced him and kissed him.

Luke 15:31–32

TLB

"'Look, dear son,' his father said to him, 'you and I are very close, and everything I have is yours. But it is right to celebrate. For he is your brother; and he was dead and has come back to life! He was lost and is found!'"

In the parable of the Prodigal Son, the brother who stayed home got angry when his brother returned. He did not know why his father welcomed his brother home, after his brother had been bad and wasted the family's money. His father explained that he loved both his sons. God loves all his children, and he celebrates when one of them comes home!

At the end of his life, Jesus went to Jerusalem. He knew he had powerful enemies, but he also had people who followed him. When he arrived at Jerusalem, people gathered to welcome Jesus. They called him a king, shouted and sang, and spread out their robes on the road. Today, many people celebrate Palm Sunday the week before Easter, to remember the Lord's entry into Jerusalem.

Luke 19:37

ERV

Jesus was coming close to Jerusalem. He was already near the bottom of the Mount of Olives. The whole group of followers was happy. They were very excited and praised God. They thanked God for all the powerful things they had seen.

Luke 22:19
GW

Then Jesus took bread and spoke a prayer of thanksgiving. He broke the bread, gave it to them, and said, "This is my body, which is given up for you. Do this to remember me."

Before Jesus died, he had one final special meal with his followers, the Last Supper. He asked them to remember him in the breaking of the bread. When we gather together at church, we remember what Jesus did for us.

At the Last Supper, Jesus foretold that someone would betray him. When Peter said that he would never betray Jesus, Jesus said that Peter would deny him three times. After Jesus was arrested and taken away, Peter was nearby in a courtyard. Three times, someone said he was a follower of Jesus. Peter got scared and denied it each time. When the rooster crowed, he realized that he had denied Jesus. He was very sorry. Sometimes, we turn away from Jesus because we are scared. Like Peter, we can be sorry, repent, and turn back.

Luke 22:61

ERV

Then the Lord turned and looked into Peter's eyes. And Peter remembered what the Lord had said, "Before the rooster crows in the morning, you will say three times that you don't know me."

Luke 23:26

GW

As the soldiers led Jesus away, they grabbed a man named Simon, who was from the city of Cyrene. Simon was coming into Jerusalem. They laid the cross on him and made him carry it behind Jesus.

Jesus was sentenced to death on a cross. Jesus had to carry his own cross, which was very heavy, through a crowd. The soldiers told Simon of Cyrene to help Jesus carry his cross. Sometimes we can help other people when they are going through bad times. We can help carry their burden, like Simon of Cyrene helped Jesus.

Two thieves were on either side of Jesus when he was on the cross. One of them mocked him. The other thief defended Jesus and asked Jesus to remember him. Jesus promised that he would. It is never too late to repent and ask God to help us.

Luke 23:42–43

GW

Then he said, "Jesus, remember me when you enter your kingdom."

Jesus said to him, "I can guarantee this truth: Today you will be with me in paradise."

John 19:30

KJV

When Jesus therefore had received the vinegar, he said, It is finished: and he bowed his head, and gave up the ghost.

Jesus died on the cross for us. We can always remember that he died to save us from our sins. When he rose again from the dead, he defeated sin and death!

After Jesus died on the cross and was buried, several women who followed Jesus went to visit his tomb. But the tomb was empty! Jesus had risen from the dead! Praise God! An angel told the women to carry the good news to Jesus' other followers.

Matthew 28:5–7

NRSVUE

But the angel said to the women, "Do not be afraid, for I know that you are looking for Jesus who was crucified. He is not here, for he has been raised, as he said. Come, see the place where he lay. Then go quickly and tell his disciples, 'He has been raised from the dead, and indeed he is going ahead of you to Galilee; there you will see him.' This is my message for you."

John 20:28

KJV

And Thomas answered and said unto him, My Lord and my God.

After Jesus' resurrection, he appeared to his apostles. Thomas was not there. He did not believe it when the others told him that Jesus was alive again. Thomas said he would not believe unless he saw and touched Jesus for himself. When the apostles gathered together again, Thomas was with them. He saw Jesus this time! Jesus told him to touch his hands and his side. At that, Thomas believed! He proclaimed his faith in Jesus, saying, "My Lord and my God."

After his resurrection, Jesus appeared to many of his followers. He had to leave to go to heaven, though, and sit at God the Father's right hand. He promised his followers that he would send the Holy Spirit, and told them to wait in Jerusalem.

Acts 1:9–11

KJV

And when he had spoken these things, while they beheld, he was taken up; and a cloud received him out of their sight. And while they looked stedfastly toward heaven as he went up, behold, two men stood by them in white apparel; Which also said, Ye men of Galilee, why stand ye gazing up into heaven? this same Jesus, which is taken up from you into heaven, shall so come in like manner as ye have seen him go into heaven.

Jesus' followers gathered together in Jerusalem. On the day of Pentecost, the Holy Spirit came upon them. The Holy Spirit gave them strength and courage to spread the good news of the gospel to the whole world! We can always pray that the Holy Spirit will come to us, too, and help us live like God wants and spread his Word.

Acts 2:2-3

ERV

Suddenly a noise came from heaven. It sounded like a strong wind blowing. This noise filled the whole house where they were sitting. They saw something that looked like flames of fire. The flames were separated and stood over each person there.

Acts 9:3–4

ERV

So Saul went to Damascus. When he came near the city, a very bright light from heaven suddenly shined around him. He fell to the ground and heard a voice saying to him, "Saul, Saul! Why are you persecuting me?"

A man named Saul hated the people who followed Jesus Christ. He hurt, or persecuted, the early Christians. God had a plan, though. He appeared to Saul in a bright light. Saul became blind! While he was blind, a Christian man named Ananias healed him and talked to him. Saul realized he was wrong. He decided to follow Jesus! His name became Paul, and he wrote many books of the Bible and spread the Word of God to many places. God can reach even the hardest of hearts!

The apostle Peter was in prison for spreading the good news about Jesus. An angel came and helped him escape! God can help us even when things seem hopeless. God can work miracles!

Acts 12:6–7

ERV

One night, Peter, bound with two chains, was sleeping between two of the soldiers. More soldiers were guarding the door of the jail. Herod was planning to bring Peter out before the people the next day. Suddenly an angel of the Lord was standing there, and the room was filled with light. The angel tapped Peter on the side and woke him up. The angel said, "Hurry, get up!" The chains fell off Peter's hands.

1 Corinthians 12:14

KJV

For the body is not one member, but many.

Just as a body has many parts, God's church, the body of Christ, has many members. In your body, each part of your body does different work. Your eyes see. Your ears hear. Your nose smells things. In the same way, in the church, different people have different talents and different ways of serving God. Some people are great preachers. Some people are great singers. Some people are great helpers. Each person can pray to discover how they can best serve God.

In a letter Paul wrote to the church in Corinth, he talked about how important love is. Love is the most important virtue. Paul said that he could speak every language on Earth, but if he didn't say things with love, he would just be making noise. He said that love was being patient and kind, loving the truth, and being loyal.

1 Corinthians 13:13

GW

So these three things remain: faith, hope, and love. But the best one of these is love.

2 Corinthians 4:7

ERV

We have this treasure from God, but we are only like clay jars that hold the treasure. This is to show that the amazing power we have is from God, not from us.

In a letter to the church at Corinth, Paul talked about spreading the good news. He explained that when we speak of the good news, we are spreading the glory of God, not ourselves. We are like clay jars, made of earth, that carry something special. We are weak, but God's power is strong.

It can be hard to know what is the right thing to do. Sometimes we are lazy and do not want to do the right thing. Sometimes it is tempting to do the wrong thing, like be mean or jealous. But the Holy Spirit can guide us to do the right thing. When the Holy Spirit is guiding us, we see the results in our lives and how we act. The fruit of the Spirit grows within us.

Galatians 5:22–23

KJV

But the fruit of the Spirit is love, joy, peace, longsuffering, gentleness, goodness, faith, Meekness, temperance: against such there is no law.

Ephesians 6:1–3

ERV

Children, obey your parents the way the Lord wants, because this is the right thing to do. The command says, "You must respect your father and mother." This is the first command that has a promise with it. And this is the promise: "Then all will go well with you, and you will have a long life on the earth."

The Bible tells us how families should treat each other. Children should listen to their parents. This is one of the Ten Commandments! The Bible also says that parents should love their children. They should gently guide them to do the right things.

Everyone has to fight against evil and temptation. God gives you armor for that fight! The Bible says that truth is like a belt, and right living is like a breastplate. Faith is a shield. The Word of God is like a sword. Whenever you are afraid, you can imagine yourself like a knight who is ready for battle, with God's armor protecting you.

Ephesians 6:13–14

ERV

That is why you need to get God's full armor. Then on the day of evil, you will be able to stand strong. And when you have finished the whole fight, you will still be standing.

So stand strong with the belt of truth tied around your waist, and on your chest wear the protection of right living.

2 Timothy 4:7

ERV

I have fought the good fight. I have finished the race. I have served the Lord faithfully.

Paul compared his work for God to running a race. He spread the Word of God even when it was hard and he got tired! We can pray to God to help us run our race, too, to keep moving towards God and heaven.

We have faith in God, even though we cannot see him. We have faith that God loves us and will take care of us. Many people in the Bible are examples of faith. Noah trusted God and built an ark even before the rain came. Abraham trusted God that he would have a son, even though he was old. Moses had faith that God would help the Israelites escape Egypt. We can try to have faith like the Bible heroes!

Hebrews 11:1

ERV

Faith is what makes real the things we hope for. It is proof of what we cannot see.

James 1:26

ERV

You might think you are a very religious person. But if your tongue is out of control, you are fooling yourself. Your careless talk makes your offerings to God worthless.

It's easy to say something mean. It can make us feel better about ourselves to put someone else down. But God does not want us to do that. Even if we do other good things, if we say mean things all the time, it makes us less close to God.

God wants to be close to you! Reading the Bible and praying can help us be close to God. The more time we spend with God, the more we will understand and love God.

2 Peter 1:2–3

TLB

Do you want more and more of God's kindness and peace? Then learn to know him better and better. For as you know him better, he will give you, through his great power, everything you need for living a truly good life: he even shares his own glory and his own goodness with us!

1 John 1:5

KJV

This then is the message which we have heard of him, and declare unto you, that God is light, and in him is no darkness at all.

God is good! God is free of darkness, and has no evil in him. When we follow God, we too live in the light and turn away from the darkness of sin.

How do we know how we should act? We can imitate the example of other people. We can read the Bible and see how the Bible heroes lived. We can also look at family members and friends who act kindly. We can try to act like them.

3 John 11

NRSVUE

Beloved, do not imitate what is evil, but imitate what is good. Whoever does good is from God; whoever does evil has not seen God.

Revelation 3:20

TLB

"Look! I have been standing at the door, and I am constantly knocking. If anyone hears me calling him and opens the door, I will come in and fellowship with him and he with me.

Jesus wants to be part of our lives. We can imagine him knocking at the door like a visitor. We can choose to lock Jesus out or to let Jesus in. When we do let Jesus in, he can help us, heal us, and bring true joy to our lives. We just need to open the door!

Revelation 4:11

KJV

Thou art worthy, O Lord, to receive glory and honour and power: for thou hast created all things, and for thy pleasure they are and were created.